LIGHT COMMERCIAL
VEHICLES

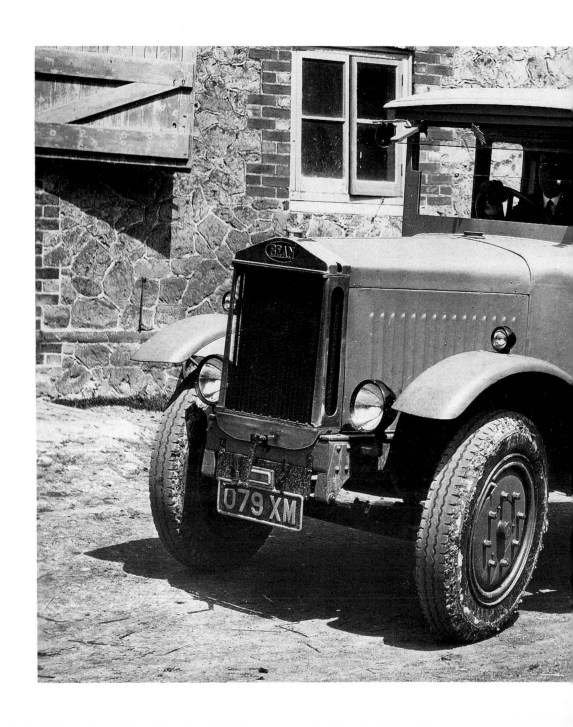

LIGHT COMMERCIAL VEHICLES

S. W. STEVENS-STRATTEN

LONDON

IAN ALLAN LTD

First published 1991

ISBN 0 7110 1949 5

Published by Ian Allan Ltd, Shepperton, Surrey; and printed by Ian Allan Printing Ltd at their works at Coombelands in Runnymede, England.

Front cover, top:
A 1966 Morris model LD 1-ton van, widely used by the Post Office. The design was introduced in 1954 and was badged as Austin, Morris or even BMC. *C. D. Jones*

Front cover, bottom:
A Walker (Chicago, USA) 1-ton battery-electric van of c1920, now preserved. It is powered by a 60 cell 72V battery which weighs 11cwt, and this drives a 4hp motor. *VRPL*

Rear cover, top:
A 1931 Morris Minor 5cwt pick-up truck, now preserved and seen at a rally at Ascot in May 1973. This version of the Morris Commercial was introduced in 1929 and remained in production until 1934. *Rex Kennedy*

Rear cover, bottom:
A 1952 Jowett Bradford 10cwt van, seen on a rally in the late 1980s. Manufacture ceased in 1954. *Adrian A. Thomas*

Contents

Introduction

Soon after the advent of the motor-car it was carrying goods and produce, thus the light delivery vehicle was a natural progression. The light vehicle is often looked upon by road transport enthusiasts with less favour than the heavy commercial vehicles which seem to attract far more interest. Yet the lighter vehicle plays just as an important role in transport generally to say nothing of the economy and welfare of the country as a whole.

Prior to World War 2 the small light delivery vans were commonplace as most local traders — the butcher, baker, fishmonger, hardware store, etc would deliver their products to their customers, sometimes on a daily basis. However, economics, plus the fact that most of the households today own at least one motor car so they can collect and transport their own shopping, have made this useful facility a practice of the past. Another factor is the rise in ownership of domestic washing machines and coin-operated launderettes, which saw the decline in the laundry services with their collection and delivery fleet.

Another sign of the times is the almost total absence of hand-painted illustrations and ornate signwriting on the sides of vehicles. Nowadays it is a case of transfers, often on a plastic base, which are stuck to the sides of vehicles, but more often than not they just have simple plain lettering proclaiming the owner — and this is often a plastic sticker!

Below:
A Hillman 6cwt van produced in 1930, just after the Rootes Group had taken over Commer. Note the square outline and the wire wheels.
Ian Allan Library (IAL)

5

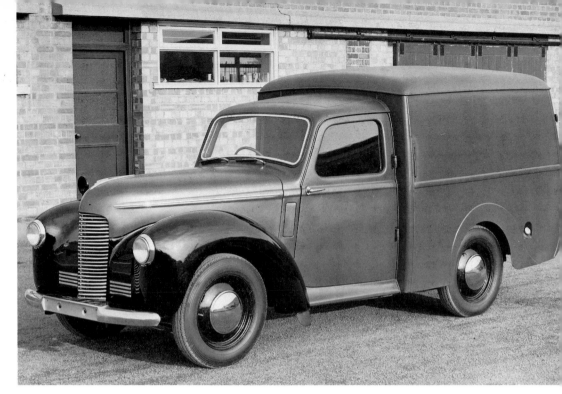

Above:
An interesting comparison with the previous illustration. This is a Commer Supervan, c1950, based on a Hillman Minx car and using the same engine and chassis. The carrying capacity is 8cwt *IAL*

Right:
A restored and preserved 1912 Rover 12hp van originally owned by a wine merchant in Derby and in regular use until 1961. It was purchased in 1970 and put into its present livery. Seen here at a rally in York in September 1988. *A. E. Peacock*

Below:
A good example of a normal saloon car — a 1935 Austin — converted for commercial use. *A. C. Mott*

A great number of commercial vehicle manufacturers never came into the lighter market, being content to make models of 3ton or over or even passenger-carrying chassis. Likewise a number of manufacturers of motorcars supplied a van body on their car chassis, designated as 'car derived' and this practice goes back to the earliest days and continues at the present time.

As the demand for greater payloads were made in the 1930s, and technology increased, plus more efficient engines became available, many of the more specialist manufacturers ceased making light vehicles as they found they could not compete with the mass produced vehicles coming off the production lines of the larger concerns. This is particularly relevant to the car derived vehicles.

It is not the intention of the author to give a complete in-depth history of the manufacturers, or list all their production models, but more to cover the period from the first real commercial models, c1904 up to the present day in general terms and to show the advances made both in appearance, carrying capacity and technical progress. We have come a long way from the local builders handcart to the modern pick-up truck. It is also interesting to see the changes in the styles of bodywork which has been employed during the period covered, not forgetting the special bodywork built for advertising purposes.

The fashion for three-wheeler vans with motor-cycle engines, in the 1930s was another phase which comes within the scope of this book, but we do not consider estate cars and shooting brakes as commercial vehicles, although some have been used for this purpose. It is also worthy of note that no light steam powered vehicles were ever produced, as far as we know not even an adaptation of a steam driven motorcar.

Some brief technical data is given, and the dimensions given in relation to the engine data refers to the bore and the stroke respectively. In some cases engines have been uprated in later versions of the same model.

A word of praise should be given to the enthusiasts who have preserved and restored some of the vehicles shown in this book, for through their hard and painstaking work they have kept alive a piece of history, one may almost say our heritage.

Photographs have been credited to the respective photographers and the following abbreviations apply — IAL = Ian Allan Library; VRPL = Vintage Roadscene Publications Ltd; and PDMC = Peter Daniels Moto'graphs Collection.

S. W. Stevens-Stratten, FRSA
Epsom, Surrey
November 1990

Below:
In 1986 Ford redesigned their popular Transit van. Here is one of the new standard models for a payload of 17cwt and supplied with a 2 litre petrol engine.
Vintage Roadscene Publications Ltd (VRPL)

Below:
**The only lightweight commercial vehicle produced
by AEC was the 201 model in 1923/4. It was
designed to run on either solid or pneumatic tyres
and had a four-cylinder petrol engine.** *IAL*

AEC

(Associated Equipment Co Ltd)

AEC was formed in 1912 by the London General Omnibus Co for the manufacture of buses in the old Vanguard Bus Company's premises in Blackhorse Road, Walthamstow. Later the company expanded and in 1927 moved to a purpose-built factory at Southall, Middlesex.

The first commercial vehicle was produced for the War Department in 1916, a 3ton Y type, and commercial vehicles then continued in production until the company ceased production in 1972, having been taken over by Leyland in 1962. They were known throughout the world as 'Builders of London's Buses', but also for rugged and reliable heavy vehicles.

They only made one light commercial vehicle, which incidentally was their first true goods chassis, and this was the 201 type introduced in 1923 for a payload of 2/2½ton, using an AEC four-cylinder 28hp wet sleeve monobloc engine. This and the succeeding 204 type remained in production until 1928 when the model was dropped from their range. During 1927 some of these models were badged as 'Associated Daimler' when AEC and Daimler underwent a temporary merger of their products for two years.

Albion

The Albion Motor Car Co was founded in 1901 by T. Blackwood Murray and N. O. Fulton (previously with Arrol-Johnson), at Bathgate, near Glasgow. The following year they produced their first light van, which was based on their model A2, a tiller-steered, opposed two-cylinder, 8hp dog-cart, which could carry a 10cwt payload. Later the engine was increased to 10hp and a conventional steering wheel provided. The dog-cart had the engine around the rear axle, so this could almost be described as the first under-floor-engined commercial vehicle!

In 1903 they introduced their A3 model, a 12hp (soon uprated to 16hp), two-cylinder chain-driven van and this design lasted until 1914, by which time their light vehicles were being manufactured for payloads from 10-25cwt, having obtained larger premises at Scotstoun in 1904.

It was in 1910 that they produced the highly successful A10 1ton models with four-cylinder 32hp engines which remained in production until 1962, chain-drive being the order of the day. However, in 1913 the normal-control A14 model, had a live axle, three-speed crash gearbox and a payload capacity of 15cwt.

After the end of World War 1 they continued with commercial vehicle production, introducing the normal-control 30cwt (later uprated to 2ton). SB24 model, which proved popular with many operators.

In the 1920s they adopted the slogan 'Sure as the Sunrise' with a setting sun motive moulded on the radiator top. The name was changed to Albion Motors Ltd in 1930. During 1926 they introduced the LA24 and LB24 chassis for 25cwt and 30cwt respectively, both fitted with a 24hp (98.5mm bore by 127mm stroke), both only remaining in production for two years. However, the LB40 and LB41 models of 1929 and 1930 for a 30cwt payload proved more successful. During the 1930s Albion produced a large number of 30/40cwt normal control vans and lorries, as well as the well known RAF ambulances which date from 1937.

After World War 2 Albion produced the AL5N and AZ5N 30cwt models with choice of petrol or diesel engines. In 1955 they introduced the 'Cain' to their range which was a lightweight version (30/35cwt payload) of the heavier Claymore (4/5ton), but the model had few sales and was withdrawn after about a year.

Albion continued to make heavier vehicles, as they had since 1919, until 1972 when they were merged into the Leyland Group, who had taken them over in 1951.

Above:
A 1904 Albion 16hp van which gives no weather protection for the driver! *IAL*

Below:
The Albion A14 model was produced from c1913 and this 15hp, 15cwt van was bodied by the London firm of E. & H. Hora Ltd with lettering and insignia probably ahead of its time. *VRPL*

Above:
This looks as if it should carry more than 30cwt, but the SB24 model of 1926 was so designed. The four-cylinder petrol engine was rated at 24hp and the chassis at 34½cwt was heavier than the payload. Seen on the Trans-Pennine Run from Manchester to Harrogate in 1971. *S. W. Stevens-Stratten*

Below:
A 2/2½ton normal control model CL122 of 1937 supplied to a Norwich operator. It was fitted with a four-cylinder petrol engine of 46hp (makers rating) — 19.6hp (RAC rating). *IAL*

Top:
The forward-control version, model CL123; of the previous vehicle. The bodywork was constructed by Scottish Co-operative Wholesale Society. Note the clerestory roof. The vehicle was supplied in January 1939. *IAL*

Above:
Albion produced the Cairn, a lightweight version of the Claymore, for payloads of 30/35cwt in 1955, but it had a short production run. The underfloor horizontal oil engine developed 55bhp and the wheelbase was 10ft. *IAL*

13

Austin

Herbert Austin founded the Austin Motor Co in 1905 and the company became one of the largest of British car manufacturers. In 1909 they produced a chassis for a commercial vehicle which was a well designed forward-control model with a payload of 15cwt.

A year later they introduced a unique model with a lattice type chassis and two propeller shafts to each rear wheel from a differential mounted at the rear of the gearbox. Its four-cylinder 20hp engine was situated below the floor and had a cast aluminium crankcase with the radiator behind the engine, which allowed a pronounced sloping front. With a payload of 2-3ton, some were in service during World War 1, but they had mechanical problems, and a 3½ton model announced in 1919 had poor sales.

Austin then ceased production of true commercial chassis, relying on van bodies on their car chassis, the Austin 7hp and the heavier 12hp being particularly used, while the 18hp and 20hp were favoured for ambulances. Bodies were built by a variety of different coachbuilders.

In 1939 Austin re-entered the commercial vehicle market with a range of vehicles from 1½ton to 3ton and known as the 'Birmingham Bedfords' for at a quick glance there was a great similarity with the bonnets and cabs of the current Bedford range. All these vehicles were to a conventional design.

In 1948 they introduced their type K8 '3-way van', a forward control 25cwt payload vehicle with a four-cylinder, 16hp (79.4mm bore by 111.1mm stroke), 2,199cc engine as used in the A70 and A90 cars. An alternative Perkins diesel was offered later. This vehicle was produced with little change until 1954.

Morris was merged with Austin to form the British Motor Corporation in 1952 and from then on models could be seen with either badge, although generally speaking Austin kept to normal control models with their original design. In 1959 the FG series was produced for 2/3/4ton models and proved popular as a medium weight vehicle for many retailers.

Above:
An early 1930s Austin 5cwt van based on the Austin Seven saloon car. *IAL*

Below:
The design of the 'Birmingham Bedfords' as they were called when Austin entered the commercial vehicle market in 1939. This is the 30cwt lorry, the design continuing after the war. *IAL*

Right:
The A40 saloon car turned up as a 10cwt van in 1949. This particular vehicle was in the fleet of J. Lyon & Co. *IAL*

Centre right:
This 5cwt van is based on the Austin A30 car, often known as the 'Coffee Pot' due to the shape of the bonnet opening! *Peter Daniels Moto'graphs Collection (PDMC)*

Below:
In 1948 Austin introduced their K8 Three Way Van, which at the time was considered revolutionary. Using the same engine as the A70 car (16hp, four-cylinder, 79.4mm by 111.1mm), it had a wheelbase of 7ft 9in and carried a payload of 25cwt. Note the wide hinged doors on the nearside for easy access which are in addition to the normal rear doors. *IAL*

Above:
The LD series of 1ton and 1½ton vehicles were usually in van form, but this example is a 1½ton truck. The drivers cab and dropside body was built by B. Walker & Son Ltd of Watford. *IAL*

Below:
This newspaper delivery van is built on the Austin FX taxi-cab chassis, which with its small turning circle makes an ideal vehicle for London streets. The wheelbase is 9ft 2⅝in while the engine is a 15.63hp petrol unit as used in the A70 series of cars. *PDMC*

Bean

The real birth of Bean Cars Ltd of Tipton, Dudley was in 1901 when
A. Harper & Sons was founded and became an established component
manufacturer for the motor industry. However, in 1909 they decided to
produce complete cars themselves which they undertook until 1929. The
company moved from one financial crisis to another and were taken over by
Hadfields, the Sheffield steel manufacturers, in 1926.

In 1925 they decided to enter the commercial vehicle market and
produced a 25cwt chassis using a four-cylinder 13.9hp engine from their
own car range, and they continued to use this engine until they ceased
production. A year later the much needed cash injection was forthcoming
from Hadfields, so in 1927 an improved 30cwt chassis was produced. This
was followed in 1929 by a 2½ton model named the Empire.

In 1931 the New Era range was introduced with such modern innovations
as electric self-starters, good lighting, wind-up drivers windows, etc.
While this range was moderately successful, the company finally folded, as
despite cost cutting they faced severe competition from Ford, Morris and
other competitors. A reconstituted company continued as component
manufacturers.

Left:
A Bean 30cwt lorry of 1930 with a 46hp Hadfield engine as used in the Bean car. The price was £325 for the complete vehicle, but it had the disadvantage of a very high ratio for the low gear. Production ceased in 1931 when the New Era range was introduced. *IAL*

Top:
A New Era 20/25cwt van which Bean produced in early 1931. It had a 13.9hp (75mm by 130mm) four-cylinder petrol engine, and had many modern innovations. *IAL*

Above:
Looking rather like a Morris Commercial of the period, this is a Bean 20/25cwt van of c1930. *PDMC*

Bedford

In 1931 General Motors decided to build their own commercial vehicles in the UK rather than import the Chevrolet range from the USA. As they already controlled Vauxhall Motors it was an obvious choice to start their new manufacturing plant at their location in Luton, Bedfordshire, hence the Bedford range was born.

The first vehicles were 2ton lorries, almost identical to the previous Chevrolets, but proclaiming 'British Bedford' on the bonnet sides. This was dropped within a year and they became a success and their slogan 'You see them Everywhere' was very apt.

In 1932 a 30cwt chassis was introduced and was redesigned in 1936, but meanwhile a light van, the BYC series for 10/12cwt payloads was introduced in 1934 and this proved popular with many retailers.

The PCV models took over the role of light vans from 1947 until 1952 when one of the most successful and popular vans was introduced. This was the CA series which at that time was an innovative and striking design. With a semi-forward-control configuration, it had a carrying capacity of 10/12cwt (later 15/17cwt models were available) and a load space of 135cu ft and it proved very popular with a production run of 17 years.

The HA series of 6/8cwt vans introduced in 1964 were based on the Vauxhall Viva car, likewise the Chevanne van of 1976 being based on the Vauxhall Chevette car.

The ubiquitous CA van was superseded in 1969 by the CF models, looking not unlike a Ford Transit, but owing much of its external design to its American counterpart, the Chevrolet.

In 1987 Bedford ceased production and was sold to AWD, apart from some small vans based on a Japanese design and titled the 'Bedford Rascal'.

Left:
The first true Bedford light van was the BYC model introduced in 1934 for 12cwt loads. It had a six-cylinder petrol engine of 19.84hp (2⅞in by 3¼in) and a wheelbase of 8ft 10½in. *PDMC*

Top:
A 1946 30cwt van used in Northern Ireland (Reg No GZ 6631), painted by Spurling Motors. The total cost of the vehicle was £502 10s. *VRPL*

Above:
A typical 30cwt Bedford van c1937 used for retail distribution. *IAL*

Top:
One of the Bedford products that epitomises their slogan 'You See Them Everywhere'. The CA van was introduced in 1947 for 10/12cwt loads. It was powered by a 12hp four-cylinder, 1,442cc engine (69.5mm by 95mm) as used in the Vauxhall Wyvern cars. The wheelbase was 8ft 9in. The Mk 1 model had a split windscreen, the later Mk II models had a one-piece screen. The CAL model looked similar but had an increased payload of 15/17cwt. *VRPL*

Left:
The CF range was introduced in 1969 with several models — CF230 for 18cwt loads, CF250 for 22cwt, CF280 for 25cwt and CF350 for 35cwt. There was a choice of petrol or diesel engines and optional overdrive and even automatic transmission was available. *VRPL*

Above:
An early example of the Bedford WS model 30cwt chassis, but with special bodywork for use as a mobile butchers shop. *PDMC*

23

Top:
The HA range of vans commenced in 1964 with a 6cwt vehicle and a 1,256cc engine, and later a larger model was also produced for 10cwt loads with a 49bhp engine. Both models were based on the Vauxhall Viva car and remained in production for many years. This is a 1979 model. *Vauxhall*

Above:
One of the last Bedford badged products was the Astra van, although this was based entirely on the Astra car, as this illustration shows it is little more than an estate car with metal panels over the windows. *VRPL*

Commer

The company was founded in 1905 by a group of businessmen under the direction of H. C. B. Underdown and produced a 4ton lorry with a unique gearbox. In 1908 they announced the HC type 2 tonner and the LC 1½ tonner, then two years later produced a BC type 30cwt chassis. However, from those early beginnings Commer only produced vehicles in excess of a 3ton payload until 1926 when Humber took over the company and light vehicles, based on Humber car chassis and engines became available. In 1927/28 a small 30cwt chassis was produced and when the Rootes Group took over Humber, Commer then produced light vans which were based on the Hillman Minx cars — a procedure which lasted until the end of Commer.

In 1931 the bonneted Commer Raider chassis was produced for 1½ton loads which proved popular both as a van or a lorry, until they were superseded by the N2 models in 1936. The Centaur models of 1933 also proved popular with many traders and operators.

An innovation of 1931 was the full forward-control Commer Pug 2ton van with a wheelbase of only 8ft. However, it was not really successful and only a few were manufactured.

In 1936 the N series was introduced covering payloads from 25cwt to 5ton and available as forward or normal-control with the option of a diesel engine for chassis of 30cwt and above.

Just prior to the war the Superpoise (or Q type) range was put on the market with models from 8cwt vans to 7ton tractive units. They were distinctive and had a well-designed appearance, but production did not get into full swing until after the war when the range proved very popular.

In 1960 a 15cwt forward control van made its appearance and was highly successful, employing a Hillman Minx engine, although a Perkins diesel was available if required. It was later designated the PB and later still the 1500 van, and was available in nine versions, standard van, high top van, milk float, bakers van, mobile shop, pick-up, mini-bus, ambulance and caravette. It was later uprated to 1ton, and used by many fleet operators including British Telecommunications. It remained as a Dodge vehicle after the take-over.

One of the most successful postwar Commer vans was the Walkthru which was introduced in 1961 and remained in production long after the Chrysler Corporation took control of the Rootes Group in 1967.

Above:
Two Commer vans of 1933, note the opening
windscreen. *IAL*

Below:
A 20/25cwt model of 1933, the chassis cost £175,
and the complete van in one primary colour was
£230. *IAL*

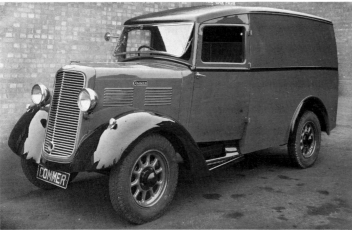

Left:
The Commer 8cwt van has always been derived from the Hillman Minx car, and this model is the 1936 version.
IAL

Centre left:
The 15cwt normal control van was manufactured for several years, using a four-cylinder 22hp (75mm by 110mm) engine. This model is from 1937. *IAL*

Below:
The forward-control 20/25cwt vans proved popular prewar, and was coded N1 model. It used the same engine as the van in the previous illustration. The colour scheme is two contrasting shades of blue with gold lettering. *IAL*

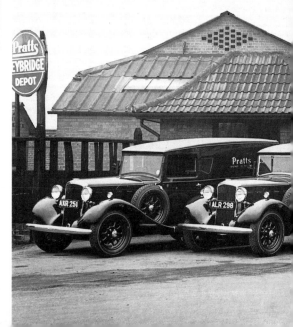

Top:
With the introduction of the Superpoise range in
1939, all the Commer range was updated, and this
is the appearance of the 30cwt van; but still using
the 22hp (75mm by 110mm) engine. *IAL*

Above:
An example of a PB or 1500 series forward-control
van for 15cwt payloads. The overall length was
13ft 11¾in on a 7ft 6in wheelbase. Later the model
was uprated for 1-ton loads. *IAL*

Left:

In 1961 Commer introduced the highly successful and very popular 'Walk-Thru' van in three capacities — 1½, 2 and 3ton, with the option of a petrol or diesel engine. The 1½ton models had a wheelbase of 10ft 3in and overall length of 17ft 1⅞in, width 6ft 9¼ in and height of 5ft 9⅜in. The smaller model can be distinguished by single rear tyres and no rear wing valences. The cost of the 1½ton was £952 complete. *IAL*

Centre left:

One of a large fleet of 30cwt vans operated by an ice cream factor. This one, purchased in 1961 has a body built by Bonallack & Sons of Basildon. It was sometimes known as the Superpoise Super Capacity Van. *IAL*

Below:

Although dated, these 1934 Commer 15cwt vans, gave an impression of a fast vehicle, as indeed they were for they used a 20hp six-cylinder engine which was also used in the largest Hillman car range. This fleet was used for petrol pump servicing. *IAL*

Dennis

Two brothers, John and Raymond Dennis started making cycles in 1885 and progressed to motor-cycles, cars and motorised lawn mowers. They made their first commercial vehicle in 1904, a 15cwt van with a four-cylinder 12hp engine, for Harrods Ltd. This was fitted with a shaft drive which was unusual in those early years. This was followed by 2ton and 2½ton trucks, as well as heavier vehicles.

Following the end of the war in 1918, the company purchased White & Poppe, the engine manufacturers of Coventry, and then marketed some lighter vehicles for 25cwt, 2ton and 2½ton as well as continuing with their range of larger models.

From 1927 to 1937 they continued to produce 25cwt, 30cwt and 2 ton chassis using a four-cylinder 17.9hp engine (85mm stroke by 120mm bore) and a wheelbase of 11ft. Originally only fitted with a three-speed gearbox, a standard four-speed box was available from 1928 and two years later the 30cwt chassis was available for forward-control if required.

In 1933 Dennis produced the first of their Ace series, or 'Flying Pigs' as they were called due to the pronounced vee shaped bonnet which protruded well forward of the front axle. A forward-control version was also produced. The payload of the Ace models was for 45/50cwt. In 1937 a normal-control Ajax model was announced for 2/3ton loads.

Two abortive attempts were made to enter the parcel collection and delivery trade with the Pazravan of 1958 and later with the Vendor but neither vehicle was successful and was soon dropped.

Dennis have consistently made many heavy duty chassis as well as bus and coach chassis in the course of their existence and were particularly known for their municipal vehicles — refuse collectors, gully emptiers etc as well as their fire appliances for which they are world famous.

Far left:
Introduced in 1925 the Dennis
30cwt model was powered
by a four-cylinder
(85mm by 120mm) 17.9hp
engine. A forward control
version was offered in 1930,
but both models were
discontinued after 1933. This
1928 van is preserved and now
owned by General Demolition
Co of Esher, Surrey.
S. W. Stevens-Stratten

Left:
K. J. Senior, well known
preservationist, fills the
radiator of his 1928 30cwt
lorry; originally owned by a
coal merchant in
Southampton. *VRPL*

Below:
From 1933-37 Dennis
produced their 45-50cwt Ace
chassis in normal and forward-
control versions. In actual fact
the name Ace was given to the
bus models, but the name
often given to both chassis
which were also known as
'Flying Pigs' because of their
pronounced snout. This
preserved Shell tanker is
showing its four cylinder
24.8hp engine at the
Weymouth Bus Rally in 1973.
S. W. Stevens-Stratten

Top:
In 1953 the Stork, an underfloor Perkins diesel-
engined chassis for a 3ton payload, was introduced.
Two wheelbase options were available, 10ft 6in or
11ft 8in. This Arlington light bodied vehicle has a
loading space of 950cu ft. *IAL*

Above:
The Heron model made its appearance in 1956.
This 2ton model has an ohv petrol engine and was
supplied in 1958. *IAL*

33

Above:
In contrast to the previous illustration is this early Dennis of c1908, ornately finished but probably only has a load capacity of 30cwt. *PDMC*

Centre right:
The Dennis 30cwt was introduced in 1925 and continued in production until 1933. This example was used by a well known store. Powered by a four-cylinder 17.9hp engine (85mm by 120mm), early models had a three-speed gearbox and rear wheel mechanical brakes plus one on the transmission. Later models were with a four-speed box. The wheelbase was 11ft. *PDMC*

Right:
The earlier model shown previously was superseded by the Light 30cwt model, but was never as popular. This box van is a good example of the forward-control type. The running units were the same as the normal 30cwt chassis. *PDMC*

Dodge

The American-owned Dodge Brothers concern produced vehicles in the USA from 1914, but did not become known in the UK until 1921 when Dodge Brothers (Britain) was founded. They commenced by importing complete vehicles and working from premises in Fulham (London). In 1927 they began assembly in a factory at Park Royal, the commercial vehicles being a 15cwt van with a 24hp engine which proved popular for retail deliveries and the newspaper trade, for it had a reputation of being fast on the road. A 1929 model being called Express or Fast Four. Some 30cwt models were also produced, badged as Grahams, a Dodge subsidiary in the USA.

When Dodge was absorbed by Chrysler in 1929 the plant was moved to the larger, existing Chrysler factory at Kew (Surrey). Production of 15cwt, 30cwt, 2ton and 4ton vehicles was soon accomplished, although still using American engines and gearboxes. However, with the new premises and increased production the first all British Dodge appeared in 1933. A 5ton tipping lorry proving very popular, likewise the 30cwt RT model.

In 1956 a full range of normal control vehicles were complemented by forward-control models. When Chrysler gained control of Commer in 1967, many of their lighter vehicles then appeared with a Dodge badge.

In the foreground is a 1933 Dodge/Chrysler 15cwt van with 21hp engine. At the rear is an early Bedford. *VRPL*

Top left:
An early 1930s Dodge 15cwt van with a Cunard built body. *PDMC*

Centre left:
A Dodge four-cylinder, 21hp, 30cwt van of 1931. *IAL*

Below:
It is interesting to see the change in appearance of this 30cwt van of 1936 which cost £255 complete. *IAL*

Right:
Supplied in late 1938 these 15cwt Dodge vans still bear a strong Chrysler influence, and it is interesting to note the bulb type horn still in use, possibly to call attention to newsboys on the streets. *IAL*

Below right:
More American in style another 15cwt Dodge van of 1939. *IAL*

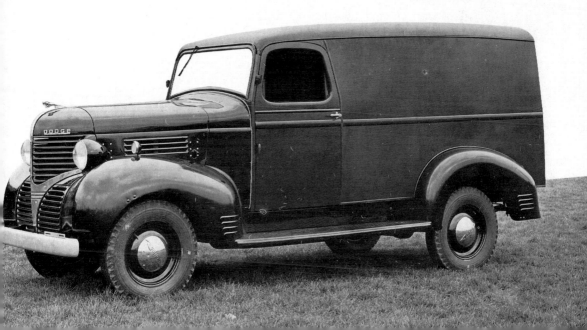

Ford/Fordson

(Thames)

The first British-assembled Ford commercial vehicle was the famous model T (also known as Tin Lizzie) which was imported complete in 1906. Henry Ford decided there was a market for his product and assembly of model Ts began at a factory in Trafford Park, Manchester in 1911. The models then continued until 1927. The model T was designed as a car but the separate chassis allowed a variety of different bodies to be fitted within the 8ft 4in wheelbase. A four-cylinder side-valve engine of 22.4hp, an epicyclic two-speed gearbox and a straight bevel rear axle was standard, although later a three-speed box was supplied. The payload was officially 7½cwt, but this was often grossly abused.

The success of the model T was phenomenal mainly due to its quality and unbeatable price, so that a larger 1ton model (wheelbase 10ft 4in) was developed using the same engine and running components, coded as model TT.

The next model was the A introduced at the end of 1927. The payload was 10cwt, the wheelbase was 8ft 7½in and it was fitted with a new four-cylinder side-valve engine of 24hp and a 3.2 litre capacity, although a smaller 14.9hp engine of 2.1 litre was also available at a later date. The AA model for 30cwt payloads using the same running units also became available at the same time.

Ford were now firmly established in the UK and the need for expansion took them to Dagenham, where on land alongside the river Thames they built a giant new factory which commenced production in 1931.

The A range was superseded by the B range in 1931/2 (models B & BF — 15 25cwt; BB & BBF — 2ton) which remained in production until 1935.

One of the most popular light vans of the era was the 1932 introduction on a Ford 8hp car, of the Y type van for 5cwt loads, and was superseded in 1939 by the E04C type, again based on the Ford 8hp car.

In 1933 all the Ford range (with the exception of the car-derived vans) were marketed as Fordson, which was changed to Fordson Thames in 1939. The Ford name on commercial vehicles was used again from 1965.

The first forward-control model appeared in 1934 as model BBE for a 2ton payload and was available with a variety of bodies and remained in production until 1938, by which time several different new models had been introduced. One of the most popular was the E83W 10cwt van which remained basically unchanged until 1957.

After the war, production continued with the 7V models introduced in 1937 for 2-5ton loads, the 566E normal-control 3 tonners. In 1961 the 400E model 15cwt van was marketed (as a Thames) and this continued until 1965 when the Transits (now marketed as Ford) appeared. This was the most popular and successful van in its class, and over the years there have been many variations.

Light 8cwt vans continued to be produced on the current private car chassis, such as the Prefect, Anglia and Escort. The Escort and Fiesta are still being produced in 1990 and like their predecessor have proved themselves as reliable and economical vehicles in their class.

Left:
One of the many model T Fords preserved. This 1920 van has some refinements not on the first models from 1908. It is pictured here at the Shareshill Fete in June 1990.
M. Matthews

Centre left:
A Ford model A van with a payload of 10cwt was produced from 1927 to 1934 and many thousands were sold. Like so many, special bodywork was constructed by coachbuilders. This shows the standard of painting and signwriting, all done by hand, which now is almost a lost art.
PDMC

Below:
The AA model made its appearance in 1927 for payloads of 20-30cwt with an option of a 10ft 11in or 13ft 1in wheelbase. The same 24.02hp (98.4mm by 107.95mm) engine as the model A was fitted. This 1929 lorry is seen at the Shareshill Fete in June 1988.
M. Matthews

Above:
A 1936 Fordson 15cwt van which was fitted with a 30hp V8 engine (77.79mm by 95.25mm) the same as fitted to the V8 cars which after the war were named Pilot. The wheelbase is 9ft 4in. *IAL*

Below:
A rear view of a 15cwt V8 van. *IAL*

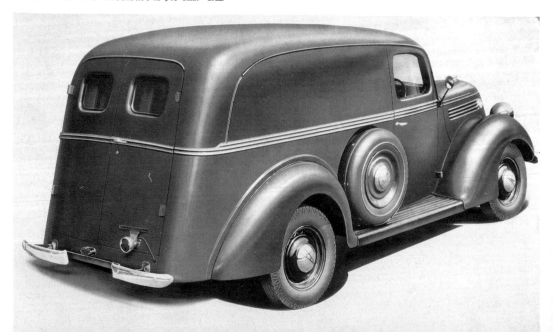

Left:
This 1936 model Y 5cwt van is based on the Ford 8hp 'Popular' saloon car. The vans were in production from 1932-37. This preserved example is seen at the end of the HCVS London-Brighton Run in 1989. *Terry A. Brown*

Centre left:
Successor to the Y type van was the EO4C using the same engine and revised radiator as on the cars. The wheelbase was 7ft 6in. *VRPL*

Below:
The Fordson E83W made its debut in 1938 and continued in production until 1957. Designed to carry 10cwt with a wheelbase of 7ft 6in it was powered by the popular 1,172cc (63.5mm by 92.5mm) four-cylinder petrol engine. A three-speed gearbox and single dry plate clutch transmitted the power to a three-quarter floating rear axle. The example shown here is a 1952 model with special bodywork. *IAL*

Above:
The ET6 model was produced in 1948 for differing payloads and with many options as to wheelbase and engines — petrol or diesel. This 1950 example is a 2ton all metal van. *VRPL*

Below:
Continuing to base their light vans on their car range this is the Thames model 300E 5cwt van, based on the Anglia saloon car, and still using the 1,172cc engine. This model was produced from 1957 to 1961. This example is sleek and well groomed! *IAL*

Top:
The forward-control Thames 15cwt van proved popular and was produced from 1958-65 and was usually in van form, this is the less common pick-up truck of 1961. *IAL*

Above:
The ubiquitous Transit van first appeared in 1965 as 12cwt and 17cwt models, but soon the range was extended up to 3½ton. There were many versions with differing wheelbases, engines and tyre sizes as well as a wide variety of bodies. Mk II versions became available in 1971. The Transit was also produced in Germany and it became one of the most successful light/medium vehicles of the 1970/80s. *IAL*

Above:
By 1968 Ford had produced the popular Escort range of cars and it was natural that a light van based on this would appear. This is the Escort 6cwt van of 1980 with a 1,100cc crossflow engine. An 8cwt model of similar appearance was powered by a 1,300cc engine. *VRPL*

Centre right:
Moving forwards the Fiesta car had its equivalent light van derivative so in 1984 we have the Fiesta L van which has three engine options — 957cc and 1,117cc petrol or a 1.6 litre diesel which is claimed to do 74.3mpg at a constant 56mph. A bit different from the model T! *VRPL*

Right:
Into the 1990s! The latest Transit model, restyled and introduced in 1986, still a market leader with many variants. *VRPL*

Garner

Started in 1914 by Henry Garner in Moseley, Birmingham the firm were importing some American-built trucks, but sold in this country under his own name, which grew to cover a range from 1½ to 6ton.

The first British-built Garner was not produced until 1925, when a 2ton model with a 24.8hp Dorman engine appeared.

New premises at Tyseley (Birmingham) enabled production to be increased and a 1½ ton and 1¾ton chassis were placed on the market. However from 1931 they concentrated on heavier models and were taken over by Sentinel in 1933, then were resold to the Dodge organisation, before becoming independent again in 1937.

A few 2ton models were then produced, but the company ceased vehicle production completely at the outbreak of the war in 1939.

Below:
A typical Garner vehicle of the late 1920s and early 1930s. This JO model is for a 3ton payload and has a four-cylinder 24.8hp engine. The body is 17ft long, by 7ft wide and 7ft high. *IAL*

The AB model for 50cwt loads appeared in 1928 with a 15.9hp (80mm by 130mm) four-cylinder engine, which may seem underpowered by today's standards. The body size is 13ft 8in long, by 6ft high. This vehicle was new in 1931. *IAL*

The second phase of Garner vehicles from 1937 produced a new and up to date cab design. This 40/50cwt lorry has a six-cylinder (3⅜in by 4½in) 27.3hp petrol engine developing 65bhp at 2,900rpm. It was fitted with Lockheed hydraulic brakes. *IAL*

Guy

Sydney S. Guy was works manager of the Sunbeam Motor Co, but in 1914 he decided to form his own company at Fallings Park, Wolverhampton. The first commercial vehicle produced was a 1½ton lorry which had a White & Poppe engine and a direct drive third gear and an indirect third (now known as an overdrive) for use when unladen, making for economic running, but with a governor restricting speed to approx 30mph.

After World War 1 several experimental innovations were made such as pneumatic springs, but this was outmoded by the coming of the pneumatic tyre. A 1¾ton and 2ton chassis was made in the early 1920s but in the main the company was engaged producing heavy lorries and bus chassis. However, from 1926-33 a 30cwt chassis fitted with a 22.5hp four-cylinder engine was available.

The production of the lighter class of vehicle was maintained from 1933 with the introduction of the Wolf 2 tonner, in forward and normal-control versions, which embodied many lightweight materials, which although adding to the initial cost was countermanded by lower running costs.

After World War 2, the Wolf was re-rated for 2/3ton payloads and all other models were for heavier carrying capacities.

In 1961 Guy was acquired by Jaguar Cars who, in turn became part of the British Motor Corporation in 1966 and was completely merged with Leyland Motors in 1968. The Guy models were then phased out in favour of Leyland vehicles.

Left:
This Guy 25cwt van was supplied in 1927 and was still in active service during the war. *IAL*

Above:
This 1934 Guy Wolf, powered by a 20hp Meadows engine has been preserved and is seen at the Guy Owners Rally at a Wolverhampton Racecourse in April 1990. *M. Matthews*

Right:
One of the first Vixen models acting as a demonstrator for the manufactures. Later Vixen models were in the 3-4ton range. Two wheelbase versions were available — 10ft 6in and 12ft 6in. *IAL*

Below right:
A Guy Wolf 2ton van with a body built by Midland Light Bodies Ltd of Coventry. It was supplied in 1934. *IAL*

Above:
By 1938 the appearance of the Wolf had changed and the familiar Red Indian was appearing as the radiator filler cap. *VRPL*

Below:
By 1939 the Wolf 2/3 tonner was also available as a forward-control vehicle. This Luton-type van has a body capacity of 1,000cu ft. *IAL*

Jowett

Ben Jowett and his brother designed their first engine in 1900 at a small garage in Idle near Bradford, and in 1906 had produced a light car with tiller steering which weighed only 6cwt. Production began in 1910, the same engine being used until 1936. This engine was a horizontally-opposed two-cylinder of 7.04hp (75.4mm by 101.5mm) which was quite economical and very robust.

Jowett launched a 5-7cwt van in 1930 with a three-speed gearbox, and this, model G, continued until 1937. In 1933 a 10cwt model was available, but neither model made much impact on the commercial vehicle market.

The Bradford van was produced in 1946, for a 10cwt payload and using a similar but uprated engine as the earlier models, Still a two-cylinder horizontally-opposed engine it now was rated as 8hp (79.4mm by 101.6mm).The wheelbase of the Bradford models was 7ft 6in for van, or lorry versions. Jowett unfortunately closed down in 1953 when they were unable to obtain bodies for their vehicles from an outside supplier.

Far left and above:
Jowett Cars of Bradford made some vans on their car chassis from 1934-40, but they made a greater impact when they introduced the Bradford van in 1946. Using a two-cylinder 81hp (79.4 by 101.6) engine, the vehicles had a wheelbase of 7ft 6in and were equipped with 16 by 5.00 tyres. These manufacturers photographs show the van and truck as they first appeared. *IAL*

Centre left:
A 1949 Bradford van used as an ice-cream sales vehicle and seen at an Austin A30/35 Rally at Top Farm near Wakefield in 1989. *A. P. Robson*

Left:
A 10cwt Jowett van c1935. It had the Jowett horizontally opposed 7.04hp two-cylinder engine (75.4mm by 101.5mm); three-speed gearbox and rod operated brakes to all four wheels. The van is owned by McNamara & Co, well known hauliers, and is on contract hire to Stearn Electric. *PDMC*

Karrier

Clayton & Co (Engineers) of Huddersfield in 1908 produced a lorry under the name of Karrier. In 1920 Karrier Motors became a separate company but were producing lorries of 3/4ton and above. However, in 1923 they produced the Z and C types for 25/30cwt loads, although it looked as though it was for a much heavier capacity, and it was uprated to 2½ton soon afterwards. A ZX model of 1½ton payload was introduced in 1926, but never proved popular. However, Karrier were starting to make a name for themselves as suppliers of municipal vehicles such as refuse collectors, gulley emptiers, etc.

In 1930 Karrier produced prototypes of a three-wheeled tractor in association with the London Midland & Scottish Railway which became known as the mechanical horse. A sideline of the production vehicles was the Colt three-wheeled trucks or vans.

Financial difficulties became apparent in 1934 and a receiver was called in, with the outcome that Karrier was taken over by Humber, already a susidiary of the Rootes Group. Production was transferred from Huddersfield to the Commer plant at Luton. As a result of this, Karrier no longer made heavy vehicles (apart from War Department contracts) and concentrated on the popular Bantam 2 tonner with a low loading height, which used some Commer components. The CK3 3/4 tonner was also produced. The Bantam remained in production from 1934 to approx 1965, although there were modifications over the years and the cab design was changed in 1948 and again in 1963.

Karrier, like Commer, was taken over by Chrysler in 1967 and badge changes between Karrier, Commer and Dodge took place, although most municipal vehicles remained as Karrier, for a few years.

Left:
An off-shoot of the Karrier Cob mechanical horse was this three-wheeled Karrier Colt. This 1932 version has a refuse collecting body. At first there were two engine options — a 7hp two-cylinder or a 9.8hp four-cylinder; but after the first year all had the later engine. *IAL*

Top:
A 1936 Colt used by Yorkshire Copper Works Ltd, Leeds. It had a four-cylinder, 1,944cc (75mm by 110mm) engine developing 13.95hp (RAC rating). The wheelbase is 8ft 8in. *IAL*

Above:
A 2ton Bantam tipping lorry supplied in 1939. It has the same engine as the Colt in the previous illustration. The wheelbase is 7ft 9⅝in. *IAL*

Right:
The Bantam continued without
change until 1950. This 1947
model is fitted with a light
alloy body. *IAL*

Centre right:
In 1951 a new Bantam model
replaced the earlier type. The
wheelbase was increased to
8ft 2in, and a new 16hp four-
cylinder petrol engine (81mm
by 110mm) was fitted. The
example here has a special
400cu ft body built by
Hoopers. *IAL*

Below:
A 1957 Bantam 2-3ton lorry in
the service of a Reading
Brewery. The platform body
measures 11ft 5in by 6ft 3in
and can carry a load equal to
1,440 pints of bottled beer!
IAL

Leyland

The origins of Leyland go back to 1880, when the Lancashire Steam Motor Co commenced building steam powered vehicles, progressing to their first internal combustion-engined vehicle in 1904. In 1907 the steam vehicle manufacturers, Couthards of Preston, were absorbed and a new company was organised under the name of Leyland Motors.

The company have always concentrated on heavy commercial and passenger-carrying vehicles, but there have been two notable exceptions, both connected with their old factory at Kingston-on-Thames. The factory was purchased to overhaul and modify the thousands of ex-WD Leyland RAF type lorries put on the market after World War 1, but when this work was finished there was a need to fill the space and Leyland then produced the Trojan vehicles from 1922-29 (dealt with in a separate chapter). When the Trojan production came to an end, Leyland introduced their lightweight Cub range, the smallest of the new models being a 2ton chassis. The first was produced in 1931 and quite an extensive range of vehicles were produced until 1940, when the factory turned its attention to munitions and other important war work.

No more lightweight vehicles carried the Leyland name until 1963, when the Standard-Triumph organisation was absorbed and the Standard Atlas vans became badged as Leyland 15 and Leyland 20 — the figure being the carrying capacity.

In 1968 Leyland merged with the British Motor Corporation and inherited the Morris and Austin range of vehicles which theoretically became Leylands.

One of the first Leyland Cub normal control 2½ton lorries to appear in 1931, model KG2. It had a six-cylinder 27.3hp petrol engine (3⅜in by 5in) and wheelbase of 14ft. *VRPL*

Left:
This 10cwt pick-up from 1974 is derived from the Morris Marina car and marketed as Austin-Morris. *VRPL*

Centre left:
Leyland made a return to the light commercial market as shown here with a 2ton van in 1964. It has a 54bhp engine and the 550cu ft all metal body was constructed and painted by Praills (Hereford) Ltd. *VRPL*

Below:
Another 2ton van of 1964. The van body was built by Norwich Coachworks Ltd and measures 13ft 3in in length, 6ft 6in wide and 6ft 6in high. *VRPL*

Morris

W. R. Morris (later Sir William, then Lord Nuffield), founded Morris Motors in 1913, and the cars quickly became very successful, some being converted to vans and trucks by outside contractors. This made Morris conscious that there was a need for a reasonably priced mass-produced commercial vehicle, and in 1924 he acquired E. G. Wrigley of Birmingham, a vehicle repairer and construction company, also the body builders Hollick and Pratt. Thus Morris Commercial Cars Ltd was founded and within six months the first mass produced 1ton truck was built, using the 1.8 litre engine from the Morris Oxford motorcar. Known as the T type, it had pneumatic tyres, electric lighting and a three-speed gearbox as standard.

The model was an immediate success, and a year later 1¼ and 1½ton vehicles were being manufactured with 2.5 litre engines and four-speed transmission plus servo operated brakes as an optional extra. The first of the D series of 30cwt and 2ton six-wheelers (6x4) with a 40hp engine were offered in 1927 and many of these were built under government contract for use with the services.

In 1933 the production was moved to Adderley Park, Birmingham which was the old Wolseley factory, taken over by Morris in 1928. The firm then entered the heavy vehicle market, even making passenger vehicles including double-deck buses for a few years, but the smaller range continued and in 1937 a successful semi-forward control 10cwt van was introduced, plus a year later the Equiload series which included the 25cwt van.

After the war the J type forward-control 10cwt van was manufactured and this proved very popular with operators of all trades, including several police forces. In 1952 Morris merged with Austin to form the British Motor Corporation and name badges changed, some remaining Morris, others as Austin and BMC. Later BMC merged with British Leyland and the Leyland badge appeared on designs which had originated from the Morris stable.

Far left:
A Morris Cowley van of c1927 after the bullnose radiator had been replaced by the flat type shown here. The payload was 12cwt and it had a 11.9hp engine. *PDMC*

Left:
Another Morris van of the 1930s based on their car chassis. The example shown here is seen at a Rally at Leyland in 1988.
Stephen Morris

Centre left:
A Morris Commercial 1ton van c1930 with a wheelbase of 10ft 2in and a 13.95 side valve engine. *PDMC*

Below:
The Morris 10cwt van series II appeared in 1936. Its semi-forward-control layout meant that the engine intruded into the cab and the driving position was offset in a cramped cab. The engine was a four-cylinder side valve unit of 1,547cc (69.5mm by 102mm) coupled to a three-speed gearbox. The wheelbase was 7ft 6in and the truck shown here is not as common as the van. *IAL*

Right:
The GPO had large numbers of the 5cwt van built from 1934-39 using the Morris Minor chassis and engine (8hp, 57mm by 90mm) and three-speed gearbox.
Adrian A. Thomas

Below:
Pleasing lines are shown on the series Y 10cwt van which made its debut in 1939. Production continued until 1942 when it was halted but recommenced from 1946-1950. It was powered by the same engine as used in the series II van. The body space is 119cu ft. *IAL*

Above:
Although designed in 1939 only a few were produced before hostilities halted production, but from 1946-52 large numbers of the series Z van were produced for a 5cwt payload. Morris used the same engine as the earlier 5cwt van. *IAL*

Centre left:
The success of the Morris Minor car applied equally to the van derivative. The 5cwt van was introduced in 1953 with the same engine and running components as the saloon. The van body has a capacity of 78cu ft, plus an additional 12cu ft beside the driver. *IAL*

Left:
Again following their car production, Morris had the Cowley van with a body of 120cu ft. This was not as popular as other models in the 1960s. *VRPL*

Above:
The J4 van was originally a Morris design from
1949 for 10cwt payloads, and was most common in
its van form. However, from 1952 when Austin and
Morris merged, it was sometimes badged as Austin
or BMC. This farmer's pick-up truck has a Jennings
body. *IAL*

Below:
A prewar model 25/30cwt van favoured by the Post
Office and many other operators which was
continued for some years after the war. *IAL*

Seddon

The firm of Foster & Seddon of Salford were commercial vehicle distributors who, in 1938, produced 6ton forward-control lorries with Perkins P6 diesel engines. They were gaining favour with operators when war was declared and the firm turned their attention to producing military trailers and other war work.

Production resumed in 1947 when the company was reorganised as Seddon Lorries Ltd with a factory at Oldham, Lancs. They continued to market the 6 tonner and expanded to become a prominent heavy vehicle manufacturer.

They entered the lighter vehicle market in 1953/4 when they introduced a normal control 1¼ton model (known as the 25-25cwt), which featured a rounded fibreglass cab. A 3ton model also appeared. The smaller vehicle did not enjoy successful sales and was discontinued within a couple of years, although the 3 tonner remained in production until 1963, mainly in the form of a short wheelbase tractive unit.

The firm took over Atkinson Vehicles in 1970 and came under the control of the International Harvester Corporation in 1974.

Below:
A Seddon 3ton Luton-type van of 1953. *IAL*

Top:
Another illustration of a Seddon 3ton model 7L supplied in 1954 to a soft drink manufacturer. *IAL*

Above:
The only real small vehicle produced by Seddon is the 25 truck, shown here with a flat bed body by Denver Motors of Leytonstone, and supplied in 1955. *IAL*

Singer

Singer Motors were motor car manufacturers, but like many others in the market had van bodies put on their car chassis. In 1929 they attempted to enter the commercial vehicle market by producing a 2ton chassis using a four-cylinder engine of 57bhp (3.1 litre) and offering a four-speed gearbox, overhead worm drive, servo assisted brakes and foot-operated lubrication. It was an advanced vehicle for its time.

A six-cylinder model, named Prosperity was produced in 1932 for a payload of 1¾ton which, like the earlier model, was using many components from the Singer motor car chassis and bodies. It was not successful and production of all commercial vehicles finished later in 1932, Singer then continuing with car production. Some of the cars were fitted with van bodies for a 1¾ton payload, often by outside contractors, until the company was absorbed into the Rootes Group in 1955.

Below:
A 1928 Singer 10cwt van which was based on the 10/26 car of the same era. It was fitted with a four-cylinder 9.8hp engine (63mm by 105mm). It is seen here at a rally at Wroughton in September 1983. *S. W. Stevens-Stratten*

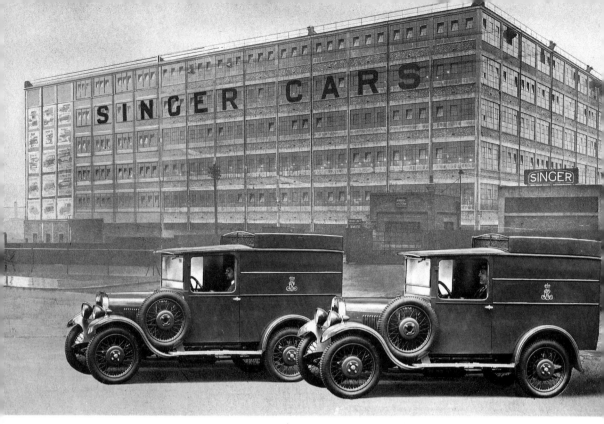

Above:
Two Singer Junior 5cwt delivery vans which were
supplied to the Copenhagen Postal Authorities in
1930. Photographed outside the Singer works. *IAL*

Below:
A 2ton Singer industrial van of 1930 used by a
London evening newspaper for fast deliveries. It
was capable of 60mph and had all the refinements
usually associated with private cars. It had a four-
cylinder 20hp engine (90mm by 120mm). *IAL*

Standard

The Standard Motor Co of Coventry became established in 1903 and were an early producer of cars. In the late 1920s and 1930s they produced for the mass market with relatively cheap and reliable vehicles, many having fabric-covered bodies. In 1931 they introduced some light vans and pick-up trucks on their 'Little Nine' car with a carrying capacity of 8cwt, and two years later increased the payload to 12cwt, which they named the Atlas 12. It would seem that these were not popular for the range was discontinued by 1935, when they concentrated on their car production, although a few car-derived 6cwt and 12cwt vans and pick-ups were available in the 1950s.

They returned to the commercial field in 1958 when they launched the Atlas name again for a forward-control 10/12cwt van, which was later uprated to 15/17cwt using the Standard Vanguard engine. The smaller model had a 948cc (63mm by 76mm) engine. The overall length was 13ft 4in, height 6ft 7¾in. It had a very tight turning circle — 29ft. Later models were supplied with a diesel engine as an optional extra. Leyland took over Standard in 1963, having had a control over them for two previous years, and some late models were badged as Leyland. Some parts of the Atlas were used by Scammell for their mechanical horses.

Above:
The prototype Standard Atlas van undergoing trials in rugged conditions before going into production. *VRPL*

Above:
A manufacturers photograph of the production
Atlas van of 1958 and although it bears the same
registration number, note that the horns have been
eliminated, presumably put inside the radiator
grille and the sidelamps have been repositioned.
VRPL

Below:
The new Standard 7cwt van with 82cu ft space
produced in 1962 and based on the saloon car. The
engine has a rating of 1,147cc. *IAL*

Top:
A van and pick-up truck of 1960 used by a well known catering concern. *PDMC*

Above:
A Standard 5cwt pick-up seen at the Eastern Bus Rally at the Royal Norfolk Showground in 1990. *D. Williams*

Thornycroft

Thornycroft was one of the oldest commercial vehicle manufacturers, the origins going back to 1864 when they established a shipbuilding business alongside the river Thames at Chiswick. With success gained in vertical water tube boilers for marine work they turned their attention to road transport and in 1896 produced their first steam wagon. They naturally progressed to the internal combustion engine, and until taken over by AEC (Associated Equipment Co) in 1961 were among the foremost heavy commercial vehicle and bus builders in the UK.

Apart from their early steam models they only entered the lighter vehicle market in 1924 with their 30cwt A1 model and two years later the A2 model for 2ton payloads. The successor to this was named 'Handy' in 1933. Another named light vehicle was the 'Bulldog' for 2½ton loads. Dandy and Nippy 3 tonners appeared at the end of the 1930s, but these were the only vehicles under 4ton produced by Thornycroft throughout their existence.

Below:
A Thornycroft 2ton Bulldog model of 1932 with a 25.6hp (RAC rating) petrol engine. *IAL*

Above:
A Thornycroft forward-control Manley 2ton van of 1933. *IAL*

Left:
Although looking as if it were for a heavier load, this Handy model is rated for 2ton capacity. The fixed-sided body has a Principality moving floor. The vehicle was supplied in 1934. *IAL*

Below left:
The same forward-control model with a van body. This looks like the 9ft wheelbase version, as against 12ft 1in or 14ft. *IAL*

Above:
During the war Thornycroft were allowed to supply vehicles to civilian operators who had a permit for essential work. This is the wartime version of the 3ton Nippy chassis. Note austerity radiator and wartime headlamp masks. The bodywork was built by Challands Ross & Co Ltd. *IAL*

Below:
The postwar Nippy 3ton van with a body capacity of 650cu ft. The panels of the body are fitted vertically and pop riveted which gives a clean surface without mouldings. The body was built by Challands Ross & Co Ltd of Nottingham. *IAL*

Trojan

The unique and unconventional Trojan car was designed by L. H. Hounsfield in 1913 and although a few were produced the war stopped further progress until 1921. A 5cwt van was produced in 1923 and this was produced by Leyland at their Kingston-on-Thames factory until 1929 when Trojan set up their own manufacturing plant at Purley Way, Croydon.

The 1923 5cwt van had 28in by 2in solid tyres on disc wheels, chain drive, a two-speed epicyclic gearbox, no self-starter and the footbrake operated on the rear wheels, while the handbrake operated on the transmission. It was of chassisless construction with a four-cylinder, two-stroke engine of 10hp (63.5mm by 120mm) situated under the front seats. In 1926 a 7cwt model was produced and this had pneumatic tyres and in 1933 a 10cwt model was marketed, the payload being increased in 1937 with a 12cwt model. However, apart from Bendix-Cowdray brakes being fitted to the latest model and the engine stroke and bore being changed in 1926 (63.5mm by 117mm) the basic principles remained the same.

When production recommenced after the war, an entirely new design for a 15cwt van was produced in 1947, but it still had a two-stroke engine, although a Perkins P3V diesel could be fitted as an alternative. In 1958 a new forward control 25cwt vehicle was produced, but this was not popular and Trojan finally ceased manufacturing in 1959.

One of the earliest Trojan vans, the sign-writing says it all! It cannot really be said that the early Trojan was an attractive vehicle! *PDMC*

Above right:
Another early Trojan van of 1924, it was registered MR 6798. *PDMC*

Centre right:
A 7cwt van of c1929 now on pneumatic tyres. Brooke Bond Tea had hundreds of this model for delivery to their retailers. *PDMC*

Below:
The postwar Trojan 15cwt van which was entirely redesigned with a four-cylinder 10.6hp (65.5mm by 88mm) engine and a wheelbase of 7ft 10in. *PDMC*

Three-Wheelers

Three-wheeled delivery vans became popular in the 1930s at a time when local retailers competed with each other to provide a delivery service to their customers. The three-wheeler, usually having the single wheel at the front, employed a motor-cycle engine and was thus very economical to operate, while the purchase price was less than a conventional van and at one time the road fund tax was less, and of course the miles per gallon was considerably increased. Many shopkeepers in towns and villages used the three-wheeler for delivering their goods, from every day provisions to such items as radio repairs and recharged accumulators, dry cleaning, hardware and most other small commodities.

Although three-wheelers in the form of 'bubble-cars' made their appearance in the 1950s and early 1960s they did not lend themselves to the carriage of goods and only the Reliant three-wheeler was available as a van, but they were never popular for their price was only fractionally lower than the basic Mini vans, which gave more comfort and stability.

There were 14 different makes of three-wheelers being produced in the 1930s, the most popular being the Raleigh who started in 1932 with a 5cwt van fitted with a one-cylinder, 598cc air-cooled engine, and in 1934 introduced a 8/10cwt model fitted with a two-cylinder, 742cc engine. The Raleigh was designed by T. L. Williams and produced by the Raleigh Cycle Co, but in 1935 the designer purchased the manufacturing rights and founded the Reliant Motor Co, which is still in existence, to continue production of the same models.

The Stevens (founded by an ex-director of AJS motor-cycles) produced a three-wheeled delivery van with a single front wheel carried in heavyweight motor-cycle forks using a water cooled side valve 588cc engine. A total of approx 500 were sold before production ceased in 1938.

The James Handyvan was a 5cwt two-cylinder 500cc model in 1932/3 increasing the capacity and power to 8cwt and 10hp in 1933, but this also ceased in 1936/7.

The Karrivan was of similar capacity but with only a single cylinder engine.

Other makers made small numbers of three-wheelers, but to no great extent.

Above:
An early motorised tri-cycle used for local deliveries. It is believed to be a c1913 Warwick Tricar for 6cwt loads with a 5.5hp single cylinder engine. They were produced in small numbers to 1935. *PDMC*

Centre left:
A 1932 Raleigh Karryall three-wheeled van with a single-cylinder 598cc engine. First used for milk deliveries in Stourport-on-Severn, and now preserved. Seen at the Dumfries & Galloway Vintage Machinery Club Rally in May 1990. *R. Kaye*

Left:
A Reliant three-wheeler of c1938 clearly showing the front forks. *PDMC*

Right:
Two preserved Reliants seen on the Trans-Lancs Rally in Heaton Park in September 1989. The leading vehicle is a 1953 10cwt model new to a London baker and following is a 1949 6cwt model originally used by a Northallerton plumber until 1974.
J. K. Grime

Below:
A 1936 James Handyvan which was found in a quarry in 1938 and now fully restored. Powered by a 1,096cc two-cylinder engine the wheelbase is 6ft 4in.   *VRPL*

Above left:
A 1939 Reliant 750cc 8cwt vehicle now preserved and seen at the Shareshill Fete in June 1990. *Mike Matthews*

Left:
By 1954 the shape of the three-wheeler had changed dramatically. This is the Reliant van of 1954. *IAL*

Below:
A newcomer to the field appeared in the late 1950s when Bond manufactured a few vans on their three-wheeled car chassis. *IAL*

Right:
The Reliant design had not stood still, this is the 1968 model TYW9 16cwt pick-up with glass fibre cab. *IAL*

Centre right:
Three-wheeled battery-electric milk floats were used in considerable numbers after the war. This 1946 version is the Brush Pony with a load capacity of 18cwt. The 30volt 160 ampere-hour battery will allow an 8-mile radius per charge. The wheelbase is 6ft 3½in. *IAL*

Below:
With a wider front and modern outline this 1961 W&E 25cwt Rangemaster Battery Electric, breaks away from the old three-wheeler look. *IAL*

Battery Electric Vehicles

Electric vehicles propelled by an electric motor fed from batteries carried on the vehicle itself are not, as many people may think, a relatively new innovation. They were in existence as far back as 1905 when the Great Western Railway built one from an American design. In the early 1920s a few were developed, but the size and weight of the batteries, which were not of the standard of later years, made them slow and gave them a restricted range before needing recharging. However, some were operated by well known London stores.

In the late 1930s improvements had been made to batteries and many small vehicles were built especially for door-to-door deliveries of milk and bread etc.

During the war, with petrol rationing, they were in great demand and used by many traders for local delivery work, including the main line railway companies. This trend continued in the immediate postwar period, but unfortunately the cost of such vehicles was often more than the conventional internal combustion-engined van which, of course, had greater speed and was not restricted in its working range.

In recent years with government and other bodies thinking of anti-pollution schemes further development has taken place, including modifying a Ford Transit to battery-electric operation. Whether this trend will continue in the next century is not known.

Left:
An early example of battery-electric traction. A 1920 Walker 1ton van used by a Kensington (London) departmental store. The electric motor develops approx 4hp on full charge. *IAL*

Above:
An Electricar of 1935 fitted with DP Kathanode batteries of 30 cells with a capacity of 196 ampere-hours giving 30-40 miles per charge. The payload is 10/12cwt. *IAL*

Right:
A Wilson electric delivery vehicle with 60volt 192 ampere-hour batteries giving a radius of approx 35 miles per charge. *IAL*

Below right:
In 1937 Selfridge & Co Ltd took delivery of several 12-15cwt Sunbeam battery electric vans, with bodywork having the appearance of early vehicles — a tradition they have maintained. *IAL*

Above:
A Midland Electric Vehicle of 1940 using 72volt batteries. *IAL*

Below:
In 1945 Northern Coachbuilders Ltd, owned by Smith's Delivery Vehicles produced battery-electric vehicles. This is a demonstration model. *IAL*

Above:
A Morrison-Electricars 10cwt
van of 1937, with a 60volt 189
ampere-hour battery. *IAL*

Right:
A 1947 long wheelbase Brush
battery-electric in use as a
mobile shop. *IAL*

Below right:
This 1950 NCB vehicle makes
an interesting contrast to the
first illustration in this
chapter. *IAL*

Above:
A Smiths NCB 1957 battery-electric used by Selfridge's for London deliveries. *VRPL*

Below:
With a cleaner environment in mind several experiments were made in the 1980s for less pollution so batteries and electric motors were fitted to several small delivery vans such as the Ford Transit and the Bedford CF show here. *VRPL*

Small Manufacturers

Above:
Belsize Motors was founded in Manchester in 1906 and ceased production in 1918. This van of unknown vintage has Beadle bodywork and was sold by Chas Baker & Co of Kent. Note the spare wheel — but no tyre! *PDMC*

Below:
Crossley Motors of Manchester are generally known as builders of buses and a few heavy commercial vehicles. However, in 1914 they built tenders for the Royal Flying Corp many of which were fitted with ambulance bodies. This is a rebodied tender now preserved and seen at the HCVS London-Brighton run in 1974. It has a four-cylinder engine of 4,531cc (101.6mm by 140mm) and a wheelbase of 11ft 4in. *S. W. Stevens-Stratten*

Above:
A 1912 Rover 12hp van which belonged to a Derby wine merchant who used it regularly until 1961 when it was preserved.
S. W. Stevens-Stratten

Left:
Beardmore Motors Ltd of Paisley, Scotland were mainly concerned with the manufacture of taxicabs, but made a few chassis for light commercial vehicles such as this 30cwt van of 1925. *PDMC*

Below left:
Traffic was an American manufacturer from 1918-29 but some of their vehicles were imported to the UK. This is a 30cwt model from c1922. Note the front chassis cross-member also acts as the front bumper. *PDMC*

Unic is a French manufacturer known in the UK for their taxi-cabs of the 1920s. This imported van is c1919 vintage. *PDMC*

Above:
Maxwell Motors of Detroit USA
were in business from 1917-23
and this 1917 1ton van was
imported to the UK and is now
preserved. It has a four-
cylinder 20.9hp engine
(3⅞in by 4½in), three-speed
gearbox and a wheelbase of
10ft 3in.
S. W. Stevens-Stratten

Centre right:
Going back to the early days of
motoring. A 1909 Renault 9hp
commercial travellers car
which even in those early days
had an interchangeable body.
It was found derelict in France
and restored in this country.
Seen on HCVS London-
Brighton Run in 1979.
S. W. Stevens-Stratten

Right:
An early Lacre 30cwt van
c1907, which illustrates the
size of such a vehicle for what
is today a small payload.
PDMC

The Unusual

Top:
The sleek lines of the Daimler ambulance chassis with a van body built by Hooper & Co
(Coachworks) an attractive but uneconomic vehicle! The six-cylinder ohv 4.095 litre petrol
engine developed 110bhp at 3,600rpm. With fluid flywheel transmission the petrol
consumption was approx 8-10mpg. The wheelbase was 12ft 6in and the overall length was
18ft 10¼in. *VRPL*

Above:
There were several 'bottle cars' about in prewar years, on several different chassis, some of
which have been preserved. This one is on a 1926 Daimler and still advertises Worthington
IPA Ale. It is seen at a Rally in Burton-on-Trent in August 1989 as part of the Midland Rail 150
Celebrations. *Mike Matthews*

Above:
It is often assumed that Rolls-Royce will not permit commercial bodies to be built on their chassis. Here are examples of two exceptions both of which have good advertising potential for the goods they carry.
PDMC

Above:
Some operators like to catch the public's eye and in the mid-1930s there was a craze for streamlining. Underneath this Robson body is a Commer chassis.   *IAL*

Below:
A small publicity unit operated by a well known Scottish Brewery. A Bedford CA van chassis with eye-catching bodywork.   *VRPL*

Signwriting and Lettering

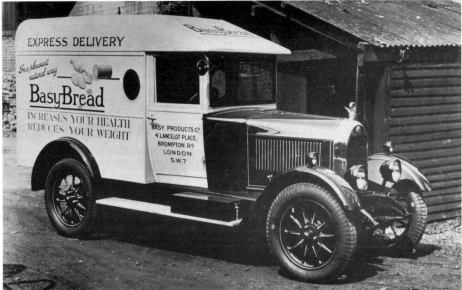

Top:
An early model T Ford with an ornate style of lettering, presumably gold shaded white. A style that is nearly extinct.   *PDMC*

Above:
A Morris van with a more modern style of lettering, but the hand and the bread are all hand-painted. c1934.   *PDMC*

Above:
An elderly Renault ice cream sales van with a perfect example of signwriting and lettering. *VRPL*

Left:
This smart 30cwt Commer van of 1938 is eye-catching and such painting on the sides of vehicles is now a lost art. *IAL*

Below left:
Looking like a 'dyed-in-the-wool enthusiasts' cap or anorak weighed down with badges this Austin A30 van was supplied in 1951, but as the operator is a manufacturer of transfers it is safe to bet they were not painted on! Nevertheless it is good publicity for the product. *IAL*

Overleaf:
What must be the epitome of good painting on the side of a vehicle. This is a hand-painted Commer van of 1970. What a pity that such works of art are now rarely seen. *VRPL*